THE RAILWAY

The change in their lives comes very suddenly. One minute they are all a happy family, with everything that they want. The next minute, Father has to go away – 'on business', Mother says. But her face is white, and the children know that it's bad news. They have to leave their nice home in London, and go and live in a little house in the country. They are poor now, Mother says. She tries to sound happy, but her eyes are sad and worried.

Roberta, Peter, and Phyllis also worry about Father, but no one can be sad all the time. A new life is beginning, with adventures around every corner. And there, down the hill from their new house, is the railway, with its shining lines leading all the way back to London; and the black mouth of the tunnel, where trains come screaming out of the darkness like great wild animals . . .

OXFORD BOOKWORMS LIBRARY

Human Interest

The Railway Children

Stage 3 (1000 headwords)

Series Editor: Jennifer Bassett
Founder Editor: Tricia Hedge
Activities Editors: Jennifer Bassett and Christine Lindop

EDITH NESBIT

The Railway Children

Retold by
John Escott

Illustrated by
Rachel Birkett

OXFORD UNIVERSITY PRESS

OXFORD
UNIVERSITY PRESS

Great Clarendon Street, Oxford OX2 6DP

Oxford University Press is a department of the University of Oxford.
It furthers the University's objective of excellence in research, scholarship,
and education by publishing worldwide in

Oxford New York

Auckland Cape Town Dar es Salaam Hong Kong Karachi
Kuala Lumpur Madrid Melbourne Mexico City Nairobi
New Delhi Shanghai Taipei Toronto

With offices in

Argentina Austria Brazil Chile Czech Republic France Greece
Guatemala Hungary Italy Japan Poland Portugal Singapore
South Korea Switzerland Thailand Turkey Ukraine Vietnam

OXFORD and OXFORD ENGLISH are registered trade marks of
Oxford University Press in the UK and in certain other countries

This simplified edition © Oxford University Press 2008

Database right Oxford University Press (maker)

First published in Oxford Bookworms 1993

12 14 16 18 19 17 15 13 11

ISBN 978 0 19 479128 1

A complete recording of this Bookworms edition of
The Railway Children is available in an audio pack ISBN 978 0 19 479100 7

Printed in China

Typeset by Wyvern Typesetting, Bristol

Word count (main text): 9295 words

For more information on the Oxford Bookworms Library,
visit www.oup.com/elt/gradedreaders

CONTENTS

1

The beginning of things

They were not railway children at the beginning. They lived with their father and mother in London. There were three of them. Roberta – she was always called Bobbie, and was the oldest. Next came Peter, who wanted to be an engineer when he grew up. And the youngest was Phyllis, who was always trying to be good.

Mother was almost always at home, ready to play with the children, or to read to them. And she wrote stories, then read them to the children after tea.

These three lucky children had everything that they needed. Pretty clothes, a warm house, and lots of toys. They also had a wonderful father who was never angry, and always ready to play a game.

There were three of them – Bobbie, Peter, and Phyllis.

They were very happy. But they did not know *how* happy until their life in London was over, and they had to live a very different life indeed.

The awful change came suddenly.

* * *

It was Peter's birthday, and he was ten years old. Among his presents was a toy steam engine, and it quickly became Peter's favourite toy. But after three days, the engine went BANG! Peter was very unhappy about his broken toy. The others said he cried, but Peter said his eyes were red because he had a cold.

When Father came home that day, Peter told him the sad story about his engine, and Father looked at it very carefully. Mother and the children waited.

Father looked at the toy steam engine very carefully.

2

'Is there no hope?' said Peter.

'Of course there's hope!' said Father, smiling. 'I'll mend it on Saturday, and you can all help me.'

Just then, someone knocked at the front door. A few moments later, Ruth – the maid – came in. 'There are two gentlemen to see you,' she said to Father.

'Now, who can they be?' said Father.

'Try to be quick, dear,' said his wife. 'It's nearly time for the children to go to bed.'

But the two men stayed and stayed. Father's voice got louder and louder in the next room, but the children and Mother could not hear what was said. Then Ruth came back and spoke to Mother.

'He wants you to go in, ma'am,' she said. 'I think he's had bad news. Be ready for the worst.'

Mother went into the next room, and there was more talking. Soon after, the children heard Ruth call a taxi, then there was the sound of feet going outside and down the steps.

Mother came back, and her face was white.

'It's time to go to bed,' she said to the children. 'Ruth will take you upstairs.'

'But, Father—' began Phyllis.

'Father's had to go away on business,' said Mother. 'Now, go to bed, darlings.'

Bobbie whispered, 'It wasn't bad news, was it?'

'No, darling,' said Mother. 'I can't tell you anything tonight. Please go *now*.'

* * *

Mother went out early the next morning, and it was nearly seven o'clock before she came home. She looked ill and tired, and the children asked her no questions.

Mother drank a cup of tea, then she said, 'Now, my darlings, I want to tell you something. Those men did bring bad news last night. Father will be away for some time, and I'm very worried.'

'Is it something to do with the Government?' asked Bobbie. The children knew that Father worked in a Government office.

'Yes,' said Mother. 'Now don't ask me any more questions about it. Will you promise me that?'

The children promised.

Everything was horrible for some weeks. Mother was nearly always out. Ruth, the maid, went away. Then Mother went to bed for two days, and the children wondered if the world was coming to an end.

One morning, Mother came down to breakfast. Her face was very white, but she tried to smile.

'We have to leave our house in London,' she said. 'We're going to live in the country, in a dear little white house near a railway line. I know you'll love it.'

A busy week followed, packing everything up in boxes. The children almost enjoyed the excitement.

'We can't take everything,' Mother told them. 'Just the necessary things. We have to play "being poor" for a while.'

On their last night in the house, Peter had to sleep on the

floor, which he enjoyed very much. 'I like moving,' he said.

'I don't!' said Mother, laughing.

Bobbie saw her face when she turned away. 'Oh, Mother,' she thought. 'How brave you are! How I love you!'

Next day, they went to the railway station, and got on a train. At first, they enjoyed looking out of the windows, but then they became sleepy. Later, Mother woke them.

'Wake up, dears,' she said. 'We're there.'

There were no taxis, and a man with a cart took their boxes. The children and Mother walked behind the cart

A man with a cart took their boxes.

5

along a dark, dirty road, which seemed to go across the fields. After a while, a shape appeared in the darkness.

'There's the house,' said Mother.

The cart went along by the garden wall, and round to the back door. There were no lights in any of the windows.

'Where's Mrs Viney?' said Mother.

'Who's she?' asked Bobbie.

'A woman from the village. I asked her to clean the place and make our supper,' said Mother.

'Your train was late,' said the man with the cart. 'She's probably gone home.'

'But she has the key,' said Mother.

'It'll be under the doorstep,' said the man. He went to look. 'Yes, here it is.'

They went inside the dark house. There was a large kitchen with a stone floor, but there was no fire, and the room was cold. There was a candle on the table, and the man lit it. Then a noise seemed to come from inside the

There was a candle on the table, and the man lit it.

walls of the house. It sounded like small animals running up and down. Then the cart man went away and shut the door. Immediately, the candle went out.

'Oh, I wish we hadn't come!' said Phyllis.

2

Peter and the coal

'You've often wanted something to happen,' said Mother, lighting the candle again. 'And now it has. This is an adventure, isn't it? I told Mrs Viney to leave our supper ready. I suppose she's put it in the other room. Let's go and see.'

They looked in the other room, but found no supper.

'What a horrible woman!' said Mother. 'She's taken the money, but got us nothing to eat at all!'

'Then we can't have any supper,' said Phyllis, unhappily.

'Yes, we can,' said Mother. 'We can unpack one of the boxes. There's some food from the old house.'

They found candles in the box, and the girls lit them. Then Bobbie fetched coal and wood, and lit a fire. It was a strange supper – tomatoes, potato chips, dried fruit and cake. And they drank water out of tea-cups. After supper, they put sheets and blankets on the beds, then Mother went to her own room.

Very early next morning, Bobbie pulled Phyllis's hair to

wake her. 'Wake up!' she said. 'We're in the new house, don't you remember?'

They wanted to surprise their mother and get the breakfast ready, but first they went to look outside. The house seemed to stand in a field near the top of a hill, and they could see a long way.

'This place is much prettier than our house in London,' said Phyllis.

They saw the railway line at the bottom of the hill, and the big black opening of a tunnel. Further away, they could see a high bridge between the hills, but the station was too far away to see.

'Let's go and look at the railway,' said Peter. 'Perhaps there are trains passing.'

'We can see them from here,' said Bobbie.

So they sat down on a big, flat, comfortable stone in the grass. And when Mother came to look for them at eight o'clock, they were asleep in the sun.

'I've found another room,' Mother told them. 'The door is in the kitchen. Last night, we thought it was a cupboard.'

There was a table in the little square room, and on the table was their supper.

'There's a letter from Mrs Viney,' explained Mother. 'Her son broke his arm and she went home early. She's coming again later this morning.'

'Cold meat and apple pie for breakfast!' laughed Peter. 'How funny!'

But their supper made a wonderful breakfast.

When Mother came to look for them, they were asleep in the sun.

All day, they helped Mother to unpack and arrange everything in the rooms. It was late in the afternoon when she said, 'That's enough work for today. I'll go and lie down for an hour, before supper.'

The children looked at each other.

'Where shall we go?' said Bobbie, although she already knew the answer.

'To the railway, of course!' cried Peter.

At the bottom of the hill there was a wooden fence. And there was the railway, with its shining lines, telegraph wires and posts, and signals. They all climbed on to the top of the fence. Suddenly, they heard a noise, which grew louder every second. They looked along the line towards the dark opening of the tunnel. The next moment, the railway lines began to shake and a train came screaming out of the tunnel.

'Oh!' said Bobbie, when it had gone. 'It was like a great wild animal going by!'

'It was very exciting!' said Peter.

'I wonder if it was going to London,' said Bobbie. 'London is where Father is.'

'Let's go down to the station and find out,' said Peter.

They walked along the edge of the line, beneath the telegraph wires, to the station. They went up on to the platform, and took a quick look into the Porter's room. Inside, the Porter was half asleep behind a newspaper.

There were a great many railway lines at the station. On one side of the big station yard was a large heap of coal, which the steam trains used for their engines. There was a white line on the wall behind, near the top of the heap. Later, when the Porter came out on to the platform, Peter asked about the white line.

'It's to show how much coal there is in the heap,' said the Porter. 'So we shall know if anybody steals some.' The Porter was smiling, and Peter thought he was a nice, friendly person.

And there was the railway, with its shining lines, telegraph wires and posts, and signals.

* * *

And so the days passed. The children did not go to school now, and Mother spent every day in her room, writing stories. Sometimes she managed to sell a story to a magazine, and then there were cakes for tea. The children did not forget their father, but they did not talk about him much, because they knew that Mother was unhappy. Several times, she had told them that they were poor now. But it was difficult to believe this because there was always enough to eat, and they wore the same nice clothes.

But then there were three wet days, when the rain came down, and it was very cold.

'Can we light a fire?' asked Bobbie.

'We can't have fires in June,' said Mother. 'Coal is very expensive.'

After tea, Peter told his sisters, 'I have an idea. I'll tell you about it later, when I know if it's a good one.'

And two nights later, Peter said to the girls, 'Come and help me.'

On the hill, just above the station, there were some big stones in the grass. Between the stones, the girls saw a small heap of coal.

'I found it,' said Peter. 'Help me carry it up to the house.'

After three journeys up the hill, the coal was added to the heap by the back door of the house. The children told nobody.

A week later, Mrs Viney looked at the heap by the back door and said, 'There's more coal here than I thought there was.'

The children laughed silently and said nothing.

But then came the awful night when the Station Master was waiting for Peter in the station yard. He watched Peter climb on to the large heap of coal by the wall and start to fill a bag.

'Now I've caught you, you young thief!' shouted the Station Master. And he took hold of Peter's coat.

'Now I've caught you, you young thief!'

13

'I'm not a thief,' said Peter, but he did not sound very sure about it.

'You're coming with me to the station,' said the Station Master.

'Oh, no!' cried a voice from the darkness.

'Not the *police* station!' cried another voice.

'No, the railway station,' said the man, surprised to hear more voices. 'How many of you are there?'

Bobbie and Phyllis stepped out of the darkness.

'We did it, too,' Bobbie told the Station Master. 'We helped carry the coal away, and we knew where Peter was getting it.'

'No, you didn't,' said Peter, angrily. 'It was *my* idea.'

'We did know,' said Bobbie. 'We pretended we didn't, but we did.'

The Station Master looked at them. 'You're from the white house on the hill,' he said. 'Why are you stealing coal?'

'I didn't think it was stealing,' said Peter. 'There's so much coal here. I took some from the middle of the heap, and I – I thought nobody would mind. And Mother says we're too poor to have a fire, but there were always fires at our other house, and—'

'*Don't!*' Bobbie whispered to Peter.

There was a silence, and the Station Master thought for a minute. Then he said to Peter, 'I won't do anything this time. But remember, this coal belongs to the railway, and even from the middle of the heap, it's still *stealing*.'

And the children knew he was right.

3

The old gentleman

The children could not keep away from the railway, and they soon got to know the trains that passed by. There was the 9.15 and the 10.07, and the midnight train that sometimes woke them from their dreams.

One morning they were sitting on the fence, waiting for the 9.15, when Phyllis said, 'It's going to London, where Father is. Let's all wave as it goes by. Perhaps it's a magic train and it can take our love to Father.'

So when the 9.15 came screaming out of the tunnel, the three children waved . . .

. . . And a hand waved back! It was holding a newspaper and it belonged to an old gentleman.

The old gentleman travelled on the 9.15 every day. He had white hair and looked very nice, and soon they were

And a hand waved back!

waving to him every morning. They pretended he knew Father, and that he was taking their love to him.

At first, they did not visit the station. After the trouble with the coal, Peter was afraid of seeing the Station Master again. But then he *did* see him, on the road to the village one day.

'Good morning,' said the Station Master, in a friendly way.

'G – good morning,' said Peter.

'I haven't seen you at the station recently,' said the Station Master.

'After the trouble with the coal . . .' began Peter.

'That's over and forgotten now,' said the Station Master. 'You come to the station when you like.'

'Oh, thank you,' said Peter.

They spent a happy two hours with the Porter.

And the three children went the very same day. They spent a happy two hours with the Porter, a nice friendly man called Perks, who answered all their questions about trains and railways.

The next day, Mother stayed in bed because her head ached so badly. She was very hot and would not eat anything, and Mrs Viney told her to send for Dr Forrest. So Peter was sent to fetch the doctor.

'I expect you want to be nurse,' Dr Forrest said to Bobbie, after he had seen Mother. 'Your mother is ill and must stay in bed. I'll send some medicine for her, but she will need fruit and milk, and some other special things that I'll write down on a piece of paper for you.'

When the doctor had gone, Bobbie showed Mother the piece of paper. Mother tried to laugh. 'Impossible!' she said. 'We can't buy all those things! We're poor, remember?'

Later, the children talked together.

'Mother must have those things,' said Bobbie. 'The doctor said so. How can we get them for her? *Think,* everybody, just as hard as you can.'

They did think. And later, when Bobbie was sitting with Mother, the other two were busy with a white sheet, some black paint and a paint brush.

The next morning, the 9.15 came out of the tunnel and the old gentleman put down his newspaper, ready to wave at the three children. But this morning there was only one child. It was Peter.

Peter was showing him the large white sheet that was

fixed to the fence. On the sheet were thick black letters that read: LOOK OUT AT THE STATION.

A lot of people did look out at the station, but they saw nothing strange. But as the train was getting ready to leave, the old gentleman saw Phyllis running towards him.

'I thought I was going to miss you!' Phyllis shouted.

'I thought I was going to miss you!' she shouted, and pushed a letter into his hand, through the window, as the train moved away.

The old gentleman sat back in his seat and opened the letter. This is what he read:

Dear Mr (we do not know your name),

Mother is ill and the doctor says we must give her these things at the end of the letter, but we haven't got enough money to get them. We do not know anybody here except you, because Father is away and we do not know his address. Father will pay you, or if he has lost all his money, Peter will pay you when he is a man. We promise it.

Please give the things to the Station Master, because we do not know which train you come back on. Tell him the things are for Peter, the boy who was sorry about the coal, then he will understand.

Bobbie Phyllis Peter

Written below the letter were all the things the doctor had ordered, and the old gentleman read through them. His eyes opened wide with surprise, but he smiled.

At about six o'clock that evening, there was a knock at the back door. The three children hurried to open it, and there stood Perks, the friendly Porter, with a large box. He put it on the floor.

'The old gentleman asked me to bring it,' he said.

Perks left, and the children opened the box. Inside were

all the things they had asked for, and some they had not –
some wine, two chickens, twelve big red roses. And there
was a letter.

Dear Bobbie, Phyllis and Peter,

Here are the things you need. Your mother will want to
know where they came from. Tell her they were sent by a
friend who heard she was ill. When she is well, you must tell
her all about it, of course. And if she says you were wrong to
ask for the things, tell her that I say you were right, and that
I was pleased to help.

There was also some wine, two chickens, and twelve red roses.

The name at the bottom of the letter was G. P. something –
the children could not read it.

'I think we *were* right,' said Phyllis.

'Of course we were right,' said Bobbie.

'I hope Mother thinks we were right, too,' said Peter. But
he didn't sound very sure.

4

Bobbie's ride

About two weeks later, the old gentleman saw another
white sheet with black letters when he looked out of the
train. It said: SHE IS NEARLY WELL. THANK YOU.

Then it was time for the children to tell Mother what
they had done. It was not easy, but they had to do it. And
Mother was very angry indeed.

'Now listen, it's true that we're poor,' she told them, 'but
you must not tell everyone. And you must never, *never* ask
strangers to give you things.'

'We didn't mean to be bad, Mother,' cried Bobbie.

'We're sorry,' said Phyllis and Peter, crying too.

Soon, Mother was crying with them. 'I'll write a letter to
the old gentleman and thank him,' she said. 'You can give it
to the Station Master to give him. Now we won't say any
more about it.'

The day after the children took the letter to the station, it was Bobbie's birthday. In the afternoon, she was politely told to go out until tea-time.

'You mustn't see what we're doing,' said Phyllis. 'It's a surprise.'

Bobbie went into the garden, and then she walked across the fields. When she came back, Phyllis and Peter met her at the back door. They were very clean and tidy, and Phyllis was wearing her prettiest dress. There was just enough time for Bobbie to make herself tidy before they called her into the front room.

Mother, Peter, and Phyllis were standing near the table, and there were twelve lighted candles on it, one for each of Bobbie's years. The table was covered with beautiful flowers from the fields and garden, and there were some interesting little boxes, too.

'Happy birthday, Bobbie!' they shouted happily. 'Open your presents!'

They were very nice presents. There was a pretty handkerchief with flowers on it, from Phyllis. A lovely little silver brooch of Mother's, shaped like a rose, which Bobbie had loved for years. There were two blue glass vases from Mrs Viney. And there were three birthday cards with pretty pictures.

'This is my present,' said Peter, putting his toy steam engine on the table. It was full of sweets. Bobbie looked surprised, because just for a moment she thought Peter was giving her the engine. 'Not the engine,' he said quickly. 'Only the sweets.' But he had seen the look on her face. 'I

They were very nice presents.

mean, not *all* the engine. You . . . you can have half, if you like,' he said bravely.

'Thank you, Peter,' said Bobbie. 'It's a wonderful present.' And she thought: 'It was very kind of Peter to give me half of his engine. Well, I'll have the broken half, and I'll get it mended.'

It was a lovely birthday. But later that night, Bobbie came silently down the stairs to get her presents. She saw her mother sitting at the table, with a pen and some writing paper in front of her. 'She's writing to Father,' thought Bobbie.

But at that moment, Mother wasn't writing. Her head was on her arms and her arms lay on the table.

'It's my birthday, and she doesn't want me to know she's unhappy,' thought Bobbie. 'Well, I won't know, I won't know.'

And she went quietly back to her room. But it was a sad end to the birthday.

* * *

The next day, Bobbie put Peter's engine in a box and took it down to the railway. She did not go to the station, but she went along the line to the place where the engines stopped.

When the next train came in, Bobbie went across the line and stood beside the engine. She had never been close to one before, and it was very big. The driver and the fireman did not see her. They were talking to Perks, the Porter, who was on the other side of the line.

'Excuse me,' began Bobbie. But the men did not hear her because the engine was making a lot of steam and noise. Bobbie climbed on to the step of the engine – but at that moment, the train began to move!

Bobbie fell inside, on to a heap of coal. 'Help!' she cried. But still the men didn't see or hear her.

'I shouldn't be here!' she thought, as the train went faster. 'I'll be in terrible trouble!'

She put out a hand and touched the nearest arm, and the driver turned round quickly. 'What are you doing here?' he shouted. And Bobbie began to cry.

This seemed to worry the two men, and they took several

Bobbie went across the line and stood beside the engine.

minutes to calm Bobbie down and to stop her crying. Then the fireman said, 'Now tell us why you're here. It's not every day a little girl falls into our steam engine!'

Bobbie picked up the box with Peter's toy engine inside it. 'I . . . I wanted to ask if you could mend this,' she explained, and took the engine out of the box. 'Everybody on the railway seemed so good and kind. I didn't think you'd mind.'

The driver took the little engine and the two men looked at it silently, not speaking for several minutes. Bobbie waited.

'What do you think, Jim?' said the driver at last. 'Can we help the little lady?'

The fireman smiled. 'I should think we can!'

'Oh, thank you!' said Bobbie.

'But now we must make sure that you get home safely,' said the driver.

Bobbie stayed on the train until it reached Stackpoole Junction. She asked the two men all about driving a steam train, and they showed her the automatic brake, and the little clock faces that told them how much steam the engine was making. It was all very interesting. At Stackpoole Junction the two railwaymen put her on another train and sent her home.

Bobbie was back in time for tea.

'Where have you been?' asked the others.

'To the station, of course,' said Bobbie. But she would not say another word.

26

It was some weeks before Bobbie took her brother and sister to meet the friendly engine driver and fireman. The two children were very surprised. And Peter was very excited when he saw his engine, now as good as new again.

And only then, as the three children walked home again, did Bobbie tell the others about her adventures on the engine of the steam train.

5

Saving the train

One day, the children were walking by the fence along the top of the hill beside the railway line. The line here ran through a deep little valley and the hillside on both sides of the line was very rocky. But among the rocks, grass and flowers grew, and many small trees.

Phyllis stood by the fence and looked down to the lines at the bottom. 'It's like looking down the side of a mountain,' she said.

Suddenly, they heard a noise. It was soft, but very clear, and slowly began to get louder.

'Look at the tree over there!' cried Peter.

The girls looked and saw a tree moving slowly downwards on the opposite side of the railway line!

'It's magic!' said Phyllis. 'I knew the railway was magic. Look, some other trees are moving, too.'

They watched as the trees moved on and on, grass and stones moving with them. Then a big rock began to move as well, and suddenly half the hillside was moving. A second or two later, everything came crashing down in a big heap on the railway line below.

Suddenly half the hillside was moving.

'It's right across the line!' said Phyllis, feeling a little frightened now.

'Yes,' said Peter, slowly. 'And the 11.29 hasn't gone by yet. We must let them know at the station, or there will be an awful accident.'

'There isn't time,' said Bobbie. 'It's past eleven now.'

They thought for a moment.

'We need something red. Then we could go down on the line and wave it,' said Peter. 'Everyone knows that red means danger, and the train would stop.'

'Our petticoats!' said Phyllis. 'They're red. Let's take them off.'

The girls did this, then the three of them ran along the line to a corner. When they were round the corner, it was impossible to see the heap of trees and rocks.

'We'll need some sticks as well,' said Peter, taking one of the petticoats. 'Now . . .' He took a knife from his pocket.

'You're not going to cut them, are you?' said Phyllis.

'Yes, cut them!' said Bobbie. 'If we can't stop the train, there will be a real accident and people will be *killed*.'

They cut the petticoats into six pieces and put them on to sticks. Now they had six red flags. Next, they pushed two of the flags into heaps of stones between the lines, then Bobbie and Phyllis each took one, and Peter took the other two. They stood ready to wave them immediately the train appeared.

It seemed a long time before the railway lines began to shake, and they heard the train coming.

'Wave your flags!' ordered Peter. 'But don't stand *on* the line, Bobbie!'

The train came very, very fast. The lines began to shake and the two flags that were pushed into the heaps of stones soon fell over, but Bobbie ran across and picked up one of them.

'The train's not going to stop!' she shouted. 'They won't see us, it's no good!'

She ran on to the line, waving her two flags.

Bobbie ran onto the line, waving her flags.

'Get back, Bobbie!' shouted Peter.

But Bobbie did not move from the line. She waved and waved her flags, shouting 'Stop, stop!' as the big black engine came towards her.

It did stop . . . but only twenty metres from Bobbie.

Peter and Phyllis ran along the line to tell the driver about the trees and rocks around the corner. But Bobbie couldn't move because her legs were shaking too much. She had to sit down on the ground.

But they had saved the train.

'You're brave and clever children,' the driver told them.

* * *

Some weeks later, a letter arrived at the little white house on the hill. It was for Peter, Bobbie, and Phyllis, and it said:

Dear Sir and Ladies – We would like to say thank you for saving the train and stopping a very bad accident. Please come to the station at three o'clock on the 30th of the month, if this is a suitable day.

J. Inglewood
Secretary, the Northern and Southern Railway Company

It was to be a very special day indeed.

The three children went down to the station at the right time, dressed in their best clothes, and the Station Master came to meet them.

'Come into the waiting room,' he said.

He took them into the room where people usually

waited for the trains – but now there was a carpet on the floor, and flowers above the pictures on the walls.

Perks the Porter was there, and several men in high hats and long coats. There were ladies in expensive dresses, and people who had been on the train on 'red-petticoat day'. Best of all, their own old gentleman was there, and he came across to shake their hands.

Then everybody sat down on chairs and an important-looking man got up to speak. He said nice things about the children – how brave and clever they were – and then he sat down. Next, the old gentleman got up and said more nice things about them. Then he called them across and gave each of them a beautiful gold watch.

Then the old gentleman gave each of them a beautiful gold watch.

'These are from the Northern and Southern Railway Company,' he said, 'to say thank you for the brave and sensible thing that you did to save the train.'

It was a wonderful day. A day that seemed more like a dream than real life.

Afterwards, the old gentleman walked with them to the little white house. 'I want to meet the mother of these clever children,' he said.

Mother was surprised to see their visitor, but she thanked him again for the things he had sent when she was ill. Then they talked about 'red-petticoat day', and the children showed Mother their watches and told her about the people at the station.

'I've been very pleased to meet you,' Mother said to the old gentleman, when it was time for him to leave. 'I'm sorry we can't ask you to come and see us again, but we live very quietly.'

The children thought this was very strange. They had made a friend – a very *good* friend – and they dearly wanted him to come and see them again.

What did the old gentleman think? They didn't know. He looked closely at Mother and said, 'I thank you, Madam, for welcoming me to your house today.'

But Bobbie was watching her mother's face as the old gentleman walked away. It was a sad, tired face.

'She's thinking about Father,' thought Bobbie.

6

A birthday for Perks

It was breakfast-time and Mother was smiling.

'I've sold another story, darlings,' she said. 'We can have cakes for tea.'

The three children looked at each other. Then Bobbie said, 'Can we have the cakes on Thursday instead of today? It's Perks's birthday on Thursday.'

'How do you know?' asked Mother.

'I showed him my brooch – the one you gave me for my birthday – and I asked him about his birthday. He says he doesn't keep birthdays any more, because he has other things to keep – his wife and children! But he said it was on the 15th, and that's Thursday.'

'And we thought we could make a birthday tea for him,' said Peter. 'He's been very good to us.'

'All right,' said Mother.

But cakes didn't seem a very exciting birthday present.

'We can give him flowers,' said Bobbie, when they were discussing it in the garden, later that day.

Then Peter had an idea. 'Perks is nice to everybody,' he said. 'There must be lots of people in the village who will want to help us give him a nice birthday. Let's ask everybody.'

Bobbie wasn't sure. 'Mother said we weren't to ask people for things.'

'Not for *ourselves*,' said Peter. 'It's all right to ask for *other* people. I'll ask the old gentleman, too.'

So they went to the village. Some people were kind, and some were not.

'It's my birthday tomorrow,' said old Mrs Ransome at the Post Office. 'Nobody will remember mine. Why should I give anything to Perks? Go away!'

But other people gave things – a pipe, a tin of tea, a walking stick – and others promised to give small presents, too.

There was a pipe, a tin of tea, and a walking stick.

Early the next morning, Bobbie and Phyllis went into the garden and cut some roses. They put them into a box with one of Bobbie's prettiest handkerchiefs. Then they wrote on a piece of paper: *For Mrs Ransome for her birthday, with our love*, and put it inside the box. Bobbie and Phyllis took the box down to the Post Office, and put it inside the door when the old woman wasn't looking.

While they were gone, Peter told his mother about Perks's presents. 'We're not doing it because he's poor,' said Peter, 'but because we like him.'

'I hope he understands that,' said Mother.

On Thursday morning, the children went to fetch the presents which other people had promised – eggs, meat, tomatoes. The old lady at the Post Office was standing outside as they went by.

'I want to thank you for the roses,' she said.

'We're pleased you liked them,' said Phyllis.

'And here's your box,' said Mrs Ransome, giving it back to them. It was now full of shiny red apples. She smiled. 'The Perks's children will like them. And I've got a pram in the back of the shop. It was for my daughter's first child, but the child died after six months. I'd like Mrs Perks to have it for her little boy. Will you take it?'

'Thank you,' said Bobbie. 'We will.'

The children put all the presents in the pram, and at three o'clock they pushed it to the Perks's little yellow house. Mrs Perks and her young children were surprised to see them.

'We know it's Mr Perks's birthday,' said Peter. 'And we've brought some presents for him.'

The woman's eyes got bigger and bigger with surprise as each thing was taken from the pram.

'Perks has never had a birthday like it!' she said.

The cakes and the presents were put on the table, then the children hid in the other room when they heard Perks

The children pushed the pram to the Perks's little yellow house.

coming home from work. They wanted to surprise him by jumping out and saying 'Happy birthday!' after he'd seen the presents.

'What's all this?' they heard him say. 'What's that pram doing here?' His wife explained, but too quietly for the

children to hear. But they heard Perks shout, 'I'm not
having any of it! We've managed all these years, asking
people for nothing, and I'm not going to start taking things
now. We may be poor, but we don't need charity.'

Bobbie ran into the other room. 'We thought you'd be
pleased!' she cried.

'We didn't mean to do anything wrong,' said Peter,
following her.

'I – I'll never be kind to anyone again!' said Phyllis,
starting to cry.

'Don't you understand?' said Perks. 'People in the
village will laugh at me. "Poor Perks, he can't take care of
his own family. We have to give him things." That's what
they'll be saying now.'

'No!' cried Bobbie. 'It's *not* charity! People were *happy*
to give you birthday presents. The man at the village shop
said, "I'm pleased to give something to Mr Perks. He
always pays his bills." And the woman at the Post Office
wanted you to have the pram. It was for her grand-
daughter, but the little girl died.'

'I'm not sending the pram back, Bert,' said Mrs Perks,
when she heard this. 'So don't ask me to.'

'I – I won't,' said Perks, quietly.

'And other people said you were kind and polite and
hardworking,' said Bobbie. 'They *wanted* to give you a
birthday present. The old gentleman gave Peter a pound for
you. He said you were a man who was good at his work.
We thought you would like—'

'Stop!' Perks said suddenly. 'I take back every word I said. I – I don't know if I was ever so pleased . . . not only with the presents, but with the kind thoughts of our neighbours. They're the best presents of all, aren't they, Nell?'

'They are!' agreed his wife, happily.

Perks looked at the children. 'You'll stay to tea, won't you?' he said.

'Oh, yes please!' they said.

7

The terrible secret

When the children first went to live at the white house, they talked about Father a lot and were always asking questions about him. But as time passed, their questions seemed to make Mother unhappy, so they stopped asking them. But they never forgot him.

Bobbie thought about Father often. She knew her mother was unhappy, and she worried a lot about that. And why was Father away for so long? Was there something that Mother wasn't telling them?

The answer came on the day she went to the station, to fetch the magazines. They were old magazines which people left on trains or in the waiting room. Perks said the children could have them to read, and one day Bobbie went to fetch them.

'I'll just put some newspaper round them to keep them together,' said Perks. And he took an old newspaper from the heap.

The magazines were heavy, and Bobbie stopped to rest on the way home. She sat on the grass and dropped them beside her. As she did this, she looked at the newspaper and read some of the words on the page . . . *and it was like a terrible dream.*

She never remembered how she got home. But she went to her room and locked the door. Then she took the newspaper off the magazines and looked at it again. The words seemed to jump at her:

FIVE YEARS IN PRISON FOR SPY!

And the name of the 'spy' was the name of her father.

Bobbie looked at the newspaper and read some of the words on the page.

Bobbie was very quiet at tea-time.

'Is anything wrong?' Mother asked her.

'I'm all right,' said Bobbie.

But after tea, Mother went up to Bobbie's room. 'What's the matter?' she wanted to know.

For an answer, Bobbie took the newspaper from under her bed and showed it to her mother.

'Oh, Bobbie!' cried Mother. 'You don't believe it, do you? You don't believe Daddy is a spy?'

'No!' said Bobbie.

'He's good and honest and he's done nothing wrong,' said Mother. 'We have to remember that.'

'What happened?' asked Bobbie.

'You remember the two men who came to see Daddy at the old house, don't you?' said Mother. 'They said he was a spy, and that he'd sold Government secrets to another country. There were some letters in Daddy's desk at his office. When the police saw them, they were sure Daddy was a spy.'

'But how did the letters get into his desk?' asked Bobbie.

'Somebody put them there,' said Mother. 'And that person is the real spy.'

'Who?' said Bobbie. 'Who put the letters there?'

'I don't know,' said Mother. 'But the man who got Daddy's job never liked him, and he always wanted Daddy's job.'

'Is he an honest man?' asked Bobbie.

'Daddy was never really sure,' said Mother.

41

'Can't we explain all this to someone?' said Bobbie.

'I've tried, but nobody will listen,' said Mother sadly. 'I've tried everything. There's nothing we can do except be brave and patient. Now we won't talk of this any more, my darling. Try not to think of it. It's easier for me if you can be happy and enjoy things.'

But Bobbie did think about it. She did not talk to Peter or Phyllis, but she wrote a letter – to the old gentleman.

My Dear Friend,

You see what is in this newspaper. It is not true. Father never did it. Mother says someone put the letters in Father's desk, and she thinks it is the man who got Father's job. But nobody listens to her. You are good and clever. Can you find out the name of the real spy? It is not Father!

Peter and Phyllis don't know he is in prison. Can you help me? Oh, do help me!

With love from your friend,

Bobbie

She put the page of the newspaper with her letter and took it to the station. Bobbie asked the Station Master to give it to the old gentleman the next morning.

Now she could only wait and see what happened.

8

The boy in the red shirt

'The boys from the school in Maidbridge are having a paper-chase today,' said Bobbie, the next morning. 'Perks thinks they'll go along beside the railway line. We could go and watch.'

There were men working on the railway line, and the children began by watching them. They almost forgot the paper-chase, and were surprised when a voice said, 'Let me pass, please.' It was the first boy from the school.

It was the first boy from the school.

'He's the "hare",' explained Bobbie. 'All the other boys are the "hounds" and they have to chase after him.'

There was a bag under the hare's arm. It was full of pieces of paper, which he dropped behind him for the other boys to follow. They watched as he ran into the black mouth of the tunnel.

The workmen watched him, too.

'He shouldn't go in there,' said one.

'It's only a game,' said another.

'Passengers shouldn't cross the line.'

'He's not a passenger.'

Then came the "hounds", following the pieces of white paper. They came down the steps at the side of the tunnel and disappeared into the darkness. The last boy was wearing a red shirt.

'Will they take long to get through the tunnel?' asked Peter.

'An hour or more,' guessed one of the men.

'Let's go across the top of the hill and see them come out the other end of the tunnel,' Peter said to his sisters.

The tunnel was cut through a hill. They climbed over stones and through narrow openings between trees, and at last they reached the very top of the hill.

'It's lovely up here,' said Bobbie, as she looked across the fields. 'It was worth the climb.'

'The paper-chase is worth the climb,' said Phyllis. 'But hurry, or we'll miss it.'

But there was plenty of time, and they had to wait at the other end of the tunnel.

44

'Look, here he comes!' shouted Peter at last.

The hare came very slowly out of the shadows of the tunnel. Soon after, came the hounds. They were going slowly, too, and looked very tired.

The hounds were going slowly, and looked very tired.

'What shall we do now?' said Bobbie.

'That's not the last,' said Peter. 'The hound in the red shirt isn't out yet.' They waited and waited, but the boy did not appear.

The children began to worry, and they climbed down to the mouth of the tunnel. But they couldn't see a boy in a red shirt.

'Perhaps he's had an accident,' said Peter. 'Let's go and look.'

The tunnel was dark after the sunshine outside, and they walked beside the line.

'If a train comes, stand flat against the wall,' said Peter. His voice sounded very different inside the tunnel walls.

'I don't like it!' said Phyllis.

'I don't like it!' said Phyllis.

There was a low noise on the railway line.

'What's that?' said Peter.

'It's a train,' said Bobbie.

'Let me go back!' cried Phyllis.

'It's quite safe,' said Bobbie. 'Stand back.'

The train came towards them, and the noise got louder and louder. Then it was screaming past, and they could feel the hot air and smell the smoke. They pushed themselves flat against the tunnel wall.

'Oh!' said the children, after it was gone.

Peter took the end of a candle from his pocket, and his hand was shaking when he lit it with a match. 'C – come on,' he said. And the three of them went deeper into the darkness of the tunnel.

The boy in the red shirt was on the ground, beside the line. His eyes were closed and he did not move when they reached him.

'Is . . . is he dead?' asked Phyllis.

'Dead? No!' said Peter.

And slowly, the boy opened his eyes. 'I . . . I think I've broken my leg,' he said. 'How did *you* get here?'

'We saw you all go into the tunnel, and then we went across the hill to see you all come out,' explained Peter. 'The others came out, but you didn't. So we came to look for you.'

'You're very brave,' said the boy.

'Can you walk, if we help you?' said Bobbie.

'I can try,' said the boy. He did try, but he could only

stand on one foot. 'Oh, I must sit down. The pain is awful.'
He sat down again and closed his eyes. The others looked at
each other.

'You must go and get help,' said Bobbie quickly. 'I'll stay
with him. You take the longest bit of candle, but be quick.'

'You must go and get help,' said Bobbie quickly.

Peter looked worried. 'Let me stay, and you and Phyllis
go.'

'No,' said Bobbie. 'You two go – and lend me your knife.
I'll try and cut his boot off before he wakes up again. Just be
quick!'

Bobbie watched their figures disappear, then put her little candle beside the boy's foot. She used Peter's knife to cut off the boot, then she looked at the broken leg. 'It needs something soft under it,' she thought, and then remembered her petticoat. She took it off and carefully put it under the boy's leg.

He woke up a few minutes later.

'What's your name?' asked Bobbie.

'Jim,' he said.

'Mine is Bobbie,' she said. 'Peter and Phyllis have gone to get some help.'

'Why didn't you go with them?' he said.

'Someone had to stay with you,' said Bobbie. 'I must put out the candle or it will burn itself out.'

'Are you afraid of the dark, Bobbie?' asked Jim, when they were sitting in the darkness.

'Not – not *very* afraid,' said Bobbie. 'But—'

'Let's hold hands,' said Jim. He put his large hand over her small one. Then they sat and waited.

Peter and Phyllis went to a farm to get help. When the two children got back to the tunnel with the men from the farm, they found Bobbie and Jim asleep.

The men carried Jim on a piece of flat wood.

'Where does he live?' asked one of them.

'In Northumberland,' answered Bobbie. 'He told me while we were waiting.'

'I'm at a school in Maidbridge,' said Jim, 'I suppose I must get back there.'

49

rl

'A doctor ought to see you first,' said the man.

'Bring him to our house,' said Bobbie. 'It's not far along the road. I'm sure Mother will say it's all right.'

Mother *did* say it was all right, although she was a little surprised at first. Then Bobbie explained.

'I'm sorry to be so much trouble,' Jim said to Mother as the men carried him in. His face was white with pain.

'Don't worry, you poor dear,' said Mother. 'You must go to bed, and I'll send for Doctor Forrest.'

Mother also sent a message to Jim's school, to tell them what had happened.

'My grandfather lives near here,' said Jim.

'Then I'll write and tell him, too,' said Mother. 'I'm sure he'll want to know. What's his name?'

* * *

After breakfast the next day, someone knocked at the front door.

'That will be the doctor again,' said Mother. She went out of the kitchen and closed the door.

But it wasn't the doctor. The children listened as Mother and the visitor went upstairs. They heard them talking, and were sure that they knew the voice of the visitor. But who was it?

After a while, the bedroom door opened and they heard Mother and the visitor come down and go into the front room of the house. Then they heard Mother calling: 'Bobbie!'

Mother was in the hall. 'Jim's grandfather has come,' she

said. 'He wants to see you all.'

They followed Mother into the other room, and there sat – THEIR OWN OLD GENTLEMAN.

'Oh, it's you!' cried Bobbie.

'How wonderful!' said Peter. 'But you're not going to take Jim away, are you? I was hoping he could stay.'

And there sat – THEIR OWN OLD GENTLEMAN.

51

The old gentleman smiled. 'No,' he said. 'Your mother is very kind. She has agreed to let Jim stay here. I thought of sending a nurse, but your mother was good enough to agree to be his nurse herself.'

'But what about her writing?' said Peter, before anyone could stop him. 'There won't be anything for him to eat if she doesn't write.'

The old gentleman smiled kindly at Mother. 'She has agreed to stop her writing for a while, and become Head Nurse of my hospital.'

'Oh!' said Phyllis. 'Will we have to go away from the white house, and the railway and everything?'

'No, no, darling,' Mother said quickly. 'The hospital is here, at this house.'

'And my unlucky Jim is the only one needing a nurse,' said the old gentleman. 'But there will be a maid and someone to cook the meals until Jim is well.'

'Then will Mother start writing again?' asked Peter.

'Perhaps something nice will happen, and she won't have to,' said the old gentleman. 'Take care of your mother, my dears. She's a woman in a million. Now, perhaps Bobbie can take me to the door?'

The two of them went outside, and the old gentleman said, 'I got your letter, my child, but it wasn't necessary. When I read about your father in the newspapers at the time, I began trying to find out things. I haven't done much yet, but I have hopes, my dear – I have hopes.'

'Oh!' said Bobbie, crying a little.

'But keep your secret a little longer,' he said.

'You don't think Father did it, do you?' said Bobbie. 'Oh, say you don't!'

'I'm *sure* he didn't,' said the old gentleman.

9

The man at the station

Life at the white house was never quite the same again. Jim's leg got better and better, and he told them stories about his school. And now Mother was not writing stories every day, she was able to teach the children their lessons.

'I wonder if the railway misses us,' said Phyllis one day. 'We never go and see it now.'

'It seems ungrateful,' said Bobbie. 'We loved it when there wasn't anyone to play with. And we've stopped waving to the 9.15, and sending our love to Father by it.'

'Let's begin again,' said Phyllis.

So the next morning, they ran down to the fence and watched the 9.15 come out of the tunnel.

'Take our love to Father!' they cried, as they waved their handkerchiefs.

The old gentleman waved from his window. And there was nothing strange about that, because he had always waved. But now . . . hands and handkerchiefs and newspapers waved from *every* window of the train, and

*Hands and handkerchiefs and newspapers waved from every
window of the train.*

smiling faces looked up at the children on the fence.

'Well!' said Phyllis.

'What does it mean?' said Peter.

'Perhaps the old gentleman told the people to wave,' said
Bobbie. But she had a strange feeling inside her, a feeling

that something was going to happen.

Lessons with Mother were difficult for Bobbie that morning. She found it hard to think about them.

'What is it, my darling?' asked Mother. 'You don't feel ill, do you?'

'I don't know,' answered Bobbie. 'Perhaps I'd feel better in the garden.'

But the trees and the flowers all seemed to be waiting for something to happen. It was one of those quiet September days, when everything does seem to be waiting. 'I'll go down to the station and talk to Perks,' she thought.

Everyone seemed to have a newspaper in their hand that morning. Several people waved theirs at Bobbie, and smiled as she went by – people who never usually waved or smiled at her. 'How strange,' she thought.

Perks wasn't anywhere on the platform, and Bobbie had only the station cat to talk to. 'How kind and friendly everybody is today,' she said to the cat.

Perks appeared when it was time for the 11.54 to arrive. He had a newspaper, too. 'Hallo,' he said to Bobbie. 'I saw it in the paper, and I've never been so pleased about anything in all my life.'

'What did you see in the paper?' asked Bobbie.

But already the 11.54 was steaming into the station, and Perks was looking in all the windows.

Only three people got out of the train. The first was a woman with three boxes of chickens. The second was a woman with a brown suitcase.

'*Oh! my Daddy, my Daddy!*' *cried Bobbie.*

And the third . . .

'*Oh! my Daddy, my Daddy!*' cried Bobbie.

That scream went like a knife into the heart of everyone on the train. People put their heads out of windows and saw the tall white-faced man and the little girl, with their arms around each other.

'I knew something wonderful was going to happen,' said Bobbie, as they went up the road. 'But I didn't think it was going to be this. Oh, my Daddy!'

'Didn't Mother get my letter?' asked Father.

'There weren't any letters this morning,' said Bobbie. 'Oh, Daddy. It really is you, isn't it?'

He held her hand and said, 'You must go in by yourself, and tell Mother very quietly that it's all right. They've caught the man who did it. Everyone knows now that your Daddy isn't a spy.'

'We always knew you weren't,' said Bobbie. 'Me and Mother and our old gentleman.'

'Yes,' said Father. 'It's him I must thank.'

* * *

And now they are going across the field. Bobbie goes into the house, trying to find the right words to tell Mother that Father has come home. Father is walking in the garden – waiting. He is looking at the flowers, but he keeps turning towards the house.

Now the door opens. Bobbie's voice calls:

'Come in, Daddy. Come in!'

GLOSSARY

brake *(n)* something that you use to stop a moving train or car

charity help or money for people who are poor or in trouble

fireman a man who keeps the fire burning in a steam engine

government the group of people who control a country

hare a small wild animal like a rabbit, with long ears

horrible very bad

hound a kind of dog which chases and catches wild animals like hares

magic something that makes strange and wonderful things happen, which nobody can explain

maid a woman who works in another person's house

paint *(n)* something wet and coloured which you use to make pictures or to change the colour of something

petticoat a kind of 'skirt' that a woman or girl wears under her dress

platform the part of a railway station where you stand to wait for a train

porter a person who works on a railway station and who carries suitcases

pram a kind of box on wheels to carry a baby in

steam a kind of 'smoke' which comes from very hot water

wave *(v)* to move a hand (or handkerchief) from one side to the other

yard a piece of hard ground near a building, usually with a wall round it

The Railway Children

ACTIVITIES

Before Reading

1 **Read the back cover of the book and the story introduction on the first page. How much do you know now about the story? Choose T (true) or F (false) for each sentence.**

1 The children live next to the railway in London. T/F
2 They have always been railway children. T/F
3 They leave London and go to live in the country. T/F
4 There are wild animals living in the railway tunnel. T/F
5 Their best friend is an engine driver. T/F
6 The family now has very little money. T/F
7 The children's father is dead. T/F
8 Their mother is unhappy but tries to hide it. T/F

2 **How much can you guess about this story? Choose answers to these questions. (You can choose more than one.)**

1 The family is poor, so what do the children do? They . . .
 a) steal things. c) make things and sell them.
 b) get jobs. d) ask strangers for help.
2 Why has the children's father gone away? Because he . . .
 a) is very ill. c) is in prison.
 b) is a criminal. d) is abroad on business.
3 What kind of adventures do the children have? They . . .
 a) get locked in a train. c) ride with the engine driver.
 b) stop a train on the line. d) see a ghost train.

While Reading

Read Chapters 1 and 2, and then answer these questions.

1 What happened to Father three days after Peter's birthday?
2 Where were Mother and the children going to live?
3 How did they travel to their new house?
4 Why did they eat cold meat and apple pie for breakfast?
5 Where did the children go the first afternoon?
6 Why didn't Mother let them have fires in June?
7 Why did the Station Master call Peter a thief?
8 What did the Station Master do about Peter and the coal?

Read Chapters 3 and 4. Who said this, and to whom? Who or what were they talking about?

1 'It's going to London, where Father is.'
2 'That's over and forgotten now.'
3 'We can't buy all those things! We're poor, remember?'
4 'I thought I was going to miss you!'
5 'The old gentleman asked me to bring it.'
6 'I hope Mother thinks we were right, too.'
7 'Now we won't say any more about it.'
8 'You mustn't see what we're doing. It's a surprise.'
9 'You . . . you can have half, if you like.'
10 'I . . . I wanted to ask if you could mend this.'
11 'Can we help the little lady?'

Before you read Chapter 5 (*Saving the train*), can you guess what the children do and how they do it? Choose some of these ideas.

1 When an engine driver suddenly falls ill, they drive the train safely to a station.
2 They get some cows off the line just before a train comes.
3 They stop a train from crashing into some fallen trees.
4 They stop a train from going into a dangerous tunnel.
5 They hold up a sheet with a warning message on it.
6 They climb a telegraph post and send a message down the wire.
7 They make some red flags and wave them at the train.
8 They change the railway signals to make the train stop.

Read Chapters 5 and 6. Choose the best question-word for these questions, and then answer them.

What / Who / Why

1 . . . did Bobbie do that was very brave?
2 . . . were the children given beautiful gold watches?
3 . . . came back to the house to meet the children's mother?
4 . . . refused at first to give anything for Perks, and why?
5 . . . did Bobbie and Phyllis put inside the Post Office door?
6 . . . did Mrs Ransome have a pram to give away?
7 . . . did the children hide in the other room?
8 . . . was Perks angry about the presents at first?
9 . . . did people in the village say about Perks?
10 . . . did Perks like best of all?

Before you read Chapter 7 (*The terrible secret*), can you guess which are the right answers to these questions?

1 Who is the terrible secret about?
   a) The children's mother   c) The old gentleman
   b) The children's father   d) Perks the porter
2 Who finds out about the secret?
   a) Two of the children   c) Bobbie
   b) All three children   d) Peter

Read Chapters 7 and 8. These sentences are all untrue. Rewrite them with the correct information.

1 The children had stopped asking questions about their father because they had forgotten him.
2 In the paper-chase the boy in the red shirt came out of the tunnel first, so the children went to tell the workmen.
3 The children had nothing to give them light in the tunnel.
4 The boy was lying on the ground because he was tired.
5 Peter stayed with Jim, while the other two went for help.
6 Jim was the old gentleman's son.
7 The old gentleman asked Mother to be Jim's teacher.
8 The old gentleman told Bobbie a secret.

Before you read the last chapter, can you guess the ending?

1 Who is the man at the station?
2 Who sees him first?

ACTIVITIES

After Reading

1 **Perhaps this is what some of the characters in the story were thinking. Which characters are they, and what has just happened in the story?**

1 'What's all this on the table? A pipe, a walking stick, a box of apples, a tin of tea . . . and there's a pram over there! What's going on?'

2 'So that's why they wanted me to look out at the station! She was only just in time. I wonder what their letter will say? Well, I must read it and find out . . .'

3 'Oh dear! She did make me jump when she touched my arm! But I didn't mean to shout at her. Now she's crying, poor little thing! But how did she get into our coal heap?'

4 'It must be hard for them, suddenly being poor and not having enough coal for a fire. They're only children, after all. I'll just give them a warning and send them home . . .'

2 **Here is a newspaper report about the accident that didn't happen. Put the parts of sentences in the right order, and join them with these linking words to make four sentences.**

and / before / so / when / who

1 _____ were walking on the hillside beside the railway.
2 There was nearly a serious accident today

3 _____ the 11.29 train came by,

4 The driver of the train saw them waving these red flags

5 _____ some trees and rocks fell down on the railway line.

6 They knew they could not get a warning to the station

7 _____ stopped the train to find out what the matter was.

8 Luckily, the rock fall was seen by three children

9 _____ they used the girls' red petticoats to make flags.

3 **When Mother first met the old gentleman (see page 33), they didn't say very much. Perhaps this is what they wanted to say. Complete the old gentleman's side of the conversation.**

MOTHER: We live very quietly. My husband is – is away.

OLD GENTLEMAN: _____

MOTHER: Yes, he is. How did you know?

OLD GENTLEMAN: _____

MOTHER: Ah yes, the newspapers. But my husband is not a spy. He never sold secrets to anybody!

OLD GENTLEMAN: _____

MOTHER: Thank you for saying that.

OLD GENTLEMAN: _____

MOTHER: No. It's better that they know nothing about it.

OLD GENTLEMAN: _____

MOTHER: I've told them that he will be away for some time, on government business.

OLD GENTLEMAN: _____

MOTHER: You're very kind, but nobody will listen. I've tried everything. All I can do now is be brave and patient.

4 There are 22 words (4 letters or longer) from the story in this word search. Find the words and draw lines through them. They go from left to right, and from top to bottom.

F	G	O	V	E	R	N	M	E	N	T	I	P	D
C	V	S	T	A	T	I	O	N	E	U	Y	A	R
H	F	I	R	E	M	A	N	G	E	N	P	S	I
A	E	G	S	T	E	A	M	I	P	N	L	S	V
R	N	N	A	R	P	M	S	N	O	E	A	E	E
I	C	A	I	B	R	A	K	E	R	L	T	N	R
T	E	L	N	P	A	S	R	W	T	I	F	G	F
Y	C	O	A	L	M	T	S	A	E	O	O	E	L
N	L	I	N	E	F	E	O	V	R	R	R	R	A
S	Y	A	R	D	P	R	H	E	A	P	M	Y	G

1 Which words from the word search are connected with trains and the railway?

2 Which six words make the names of four jobs connected with the railway?

5 Look at the word search again and write down all the letters that don't have a line through them. Begin with the first line and go across each line to the end. You should have 23 letters, which will make 6 words.

1 What are the words, where were they, and who read them?

2 How did the person feel after reading the words, and why?

3 What did the person do after reading the words?

6 **What did the old gentleman say to the other passengers on the 9.15 on that September morning? Use words from the story (one word for each gap) to complete what he says.**

'Would you do something for me today, just after the train comes out of the _____? If you see three children, waiting by the _____, waving their _____, could you _____ back at them? You see, it's a special day for them. Their _____, who will be on the 11.54 train, has just come out of _____. He was sent there for selling _____ secrets to another _____, but he didn't do it. The police have now caught the real _____, and so this man can go home to his _____ and _____. They don't know he's coming, so it will be a wonderful _____!'

7 **What are these things usually used for? What did the children use them for in the story? Write sentences to explain.**

1 A sheet _____
2 Paint _____
3 A petticoat _____
4 A pram _____

8 **What did you think about this story? Choose some of these sentences and complete them in your own words.**

1 I *liked* / *didn't* like _____ because _____.
2 I thought _____ was *right* / *wrong* to _____.
3 I felt sorry for _____ *when* / *because* _____.
4 The part of the story I liked *most* / *least* was _____.
5 I *liked* / *didn't like* the ending because _____.

ABOUT THE AUTHOR

Edith Nesbit was born in London in 1858, but spent many of her early years in France and Germany. She did not like school – she tried to run away from one of them – but she loved reading, and read every book that she could find. The family returned to England, and in 1880 Edith married Hubert Bland. When Hubert became ill, and a business friend ran away with all his money, Edith had to work to make money for them both, so she wrote poems and stories for newspapers.

She went on writing all her life, which was a very busy one. She had five children (two of them were adopted), and she was a very 'modern' woman for the times. She cut her hair short, wore woollen clothes, and helped to start the Fabian Society (a political group). In 1899 she and Hubert moved to Kent, to a beautiful old house called Well Hall, which Edith loved. There, the Blands became famous for their weekend house-parties, which included many well-known writers. Hubert died in 1914, and Edith's life became very unhappy for a while, but later she married again. She died in Kent in 1924.

Edith Nesbit herself said she was 'a child in a grown-up world', and in her writing she never forgot what it was like to be a child – the happy moments, the fears and the worries, and the excitement of adventures. Her famous books for children include *The Story of the Treasure Seekers* (1899), *Five Children and It* (1902), *The Phoenix and the Carpet* (1904), and *The Railway Children* (1906), a much-loved story which has been filmed many times.

OXFORD BOOKWORMS LIBRARY

Classics • Crime & Mystery • Factfiles • Fantasy & Horror
Human Interest • Playscripts • Thriller & Adventure
True Stories • World Stories

The OXFORD BOOKWORMS LIBRARY provides enjoyable reading in English, with a wide range of classic and modern fiction, non-fiction, and plays. It includes original and adapted texts in seven carefully graded language stages, which take learners from beginner to advanced level. An overview is given on the next pages.

All Stage 1 titles are available as audio recordings, as well as over eighty other titles from Starter to Stage 6. All Starters and many titles at Stages 1 to 4 are specially recommended for younger learners. Every Bookworm is illustrated, and Starters and Factfiles have full-colour illustrations.

The OXFORD BOOKWORMS LIBRARY also offers extensive support. Each book contains an introduction to the story, notes about the author, a glossary, and activities. Additional resources include tests and worksheets, and answers for these and for the activities in the books. There is advice on running a class library, using audio recordings, and the many ways of using Oxford Bookworms in reading programmes. Resource materials are available on the website <www.oup.com/elt/gradedreaders>.

The *Oxford Bookworms Collection* is a series for advanced learners. It consists of volumes of short stories by well-known authors, both classic and modern. Texts are not abridged or adapted in any way, but carefully selected to be accessible to the advanced student.

You can find details and a full list of titles in the *Oxford Bookworms Library Catalogue* and *Oxford English Language Teaching Catalogues*, and on the website <www.oup.com/elt/gradedreaders>.

THE OXFORD BOOKWORMS LIBRARY
GRADING AND SAMPLE EXTRACTS

STARTER • 250 HEADWORDS

present simple – present continuous – imperative –
can/cannot, must – going to (future) – simple gerunds ...

Her phone is ringing – but where is it?

Sally gets out of bed and looks in her bag. No phone. She looks under the bed. No phone. Then she looks behind the door. There is her phone. Sally picks up her phone and answers it. ***Sally's Phone***

STAGE 1 • 400 HEADWORDS

... past simple – coordination with *and, but, or* –
subordination with *before, after, when, because, so* ...

I knew him in Persia. He was a famous builder and I worked with him there. For a time I was his friend, but not for long. When he came to Paris, I came after him – I wanted to watch him. He was a very clever, very dangerous man. ***The Phantom of the Opera***

STAGE 2 • 700 HEADWORDS

... present perfect – *will* (future) – *(don't) have to, must not, could* –
comparison of adjectives – simple *if* clauses – past continuous –
tag questions – *ask/tell* + infinitive ...

While I was writing these words in my diary, I decided what to do. I must try to escape. I shall try to get down the wall outside. The window is high above the ground, but I have to try. I shall take some of the gold with me – if I escape, perhaps it will be helpful later. ***Dracula***

... should, may – present perfect continuous – *used to* – past perfect –
causative – relative clauses – indirect statements ...

Of course, it was most important that no one should see
Colin, Mary, or Dickon entering the secret garden. So Colin
gave orders to the gardeners that they must all keep away
from that part of the garden in future. *The Secret Garden*

STAGE 4 • 1400 HEADWORDS

... past perfect continuous – passive (simple forms) –
would conditional clauses – indirect questions –
relatives with *where/when* – gerunds after prepositions/phrases ...

I was glad. Now Hyde could not show his face to the world
again. If he did, every honest man in London would be proud
to report him to the police. *Dr Jekyll and Mr Hyde*

STAGE 5 • 1800 HEADWORDS

... future continuous – future perfect –
passive (modals, continuous forms) –
would have conditional clauses – modals + perfect infinitive ...

If he had spoken Estella's name, I would have hit him. I was so
angry with him, and so depressed about my future, that I could
not eat the breakfast. Instead I went straight to the old house.
Great Expectations

STAGE 6 • 2500 HEADWORDS

... passive (infinitives, gerunds) – advanced modal meanings –
clauses of concession, condition

When I stepped up to the piano, I was confident. It was as if I
knew that the prodigy side of me really did exist. And when I
started to play, I was so caught up in how lovely I looked that
I didn't worry how I would sound. *The Joy Luck Club*

BOOKWORMS • HUMAN INTEREST • STAGE 3
The Secret Garden

FRANCES HODGSON BURNETT

Retold by Clare West

Little Mary Lennox is a bad-tempered, disagreeable child. When her parents die in India, she is sent back to England to live with her uncle in a big, lonely, old house.

There is nothing to do all day except walk in the gardens – and watch the robin flying over the high walls of the secret garden . . . which has been locked for ten years. And no one has the key.

BOOKWORMS • CLASSICS • STAGE 3
The Wind in the Willows

KENNETH GRAHAME

Retold by Jennifer Bassett

Down by the river bank, where the wind whispers through the willow trees, is a very pleasant place to have a lunch party with a few friends. But life is not always so peaceful for the Mole and the Water Rat. There is the time, for example, when Toad gets interested in motor-cars – goes mad about them in fact . . .

The story of the adventures of Mole, Rat, Badger, and Toad has been loved by young and old for almost a hundred years.